Blessings Flow

PAMELA GRAF SHORT
ILLUSTRATED BY GWEN M. STAMM

Gwen M. Stamm, *Illustrator*

www.blessingsflow.art

Library of Congress Control Number: 2021901261
International Standard Book Number: 978-1-7364233-1-8

We are grateful for the blessings that have flowed our way through the help of:
S. David Garber, *copy editor*
Robert N. Eby, *copy editor*
LuAnn Stuckey, *copy editor*
Judith Rempel Smucker, *design consultant*
Valerie J. Schrock, *web designer*
Melissa Rupp, *years of faithful prayers*

The mixed media illustrations in this book were based on stock images from these sources:
Page 5 Cynthia Thomas-Rustin, host of Gospel Dance | International Fit Dance, Inc.
Page 6-7 SWNS.com
Page 9 © Dzmitry Marhun | dreamstime.com
Page 11 519649726 | People Images | Getty Images
Page 13 Steve Gibson Design | valuestockphoto.com
Page 17 Yazolino Girl | Getty Images | iStockphoto
Page 19 CroMary | shutterstock.com
Page 21 Annie Otzen | Getty Images
Page 23 Alena Haurylik | shutterstock.com
Page 25 © Konrad Bak | 123RF.com

Printed in the United States of America
Mennonite Press
Newton, Kansas 67114

From Pamela

Lou Ann Merillat
Whose unconditional acceptance
touched our neighborhood
with grace

From Gwen

In honor of
the precious, sparkly jewel
that lives and dazzles within each one of us,
no matter our age.
Let it shine!

May our *Hopeful God* stitch you whole as a *Seamstress*, fashions a robe and cover you with honor and might

LIKE THE WATERS
ALL OVER THE GLOBE.

May our
Calling God
sing your name
as a Child
invites a friend
and whistle and wonder
and watch with you

As grace comes round the bend.

May our
Graceful God
release your sin
as a Maid
shakes out a rug
and shoo off the dust
and set you down

AND settle you
with a tug.

May our
Saving God
restore your
strength
As a Newborn
livens old ones
and splash with water,
mystery, and light,

MAKING YOU
ONE OF THE BOLD ONES.

May our
Hovering God
pause over
your gloom
as a Rainfall
strokes a rose
and catch your tears
in a bottle of gold

Wiping sorrow from your nose.

May our Powerful God Wind free your spirit as a lifts up a bird and swirl above and in and through you

With a simple

hopeful word,

May our
Healing God
wash clean
your wounds
as a Nurse
wipes down a child
and gently hold
your sacred self

IN DIGNITY
STRONG AND MILD.

May our
Gathering God
Welcome you home
as a Granny
embraces her kin
and roll out a feast
with laughter sweet

AS JOY
ABOUNDS WITHIN.

May our
Peaceful God
fill up
your frame
as a Gardener
heaps a bowl
and grow you as
a healing vine

With justice for each soul.

May our
Joyful God
anoint you
with mirth
as a Little One
giggles with glee
and soak your heart
with glory and grace

LIKE A SMOOTH
AND TASTY TEA.

May our
Believing God
quick spark
your mind
as a Reader
delights in a page
and with each sound
call you to life

Once Upon a Time

With the wisdom of a sage.

May our Devoted God remember your world as a Lover longs for home and come again with trumpet song

TO REVIVE YOUR holy POEM.

MAY God bless you
and keep you.

May God's face shine upon you
and be gracious to you.

May God look kindly upon you
and give you peace.

Numbers 6:24–26

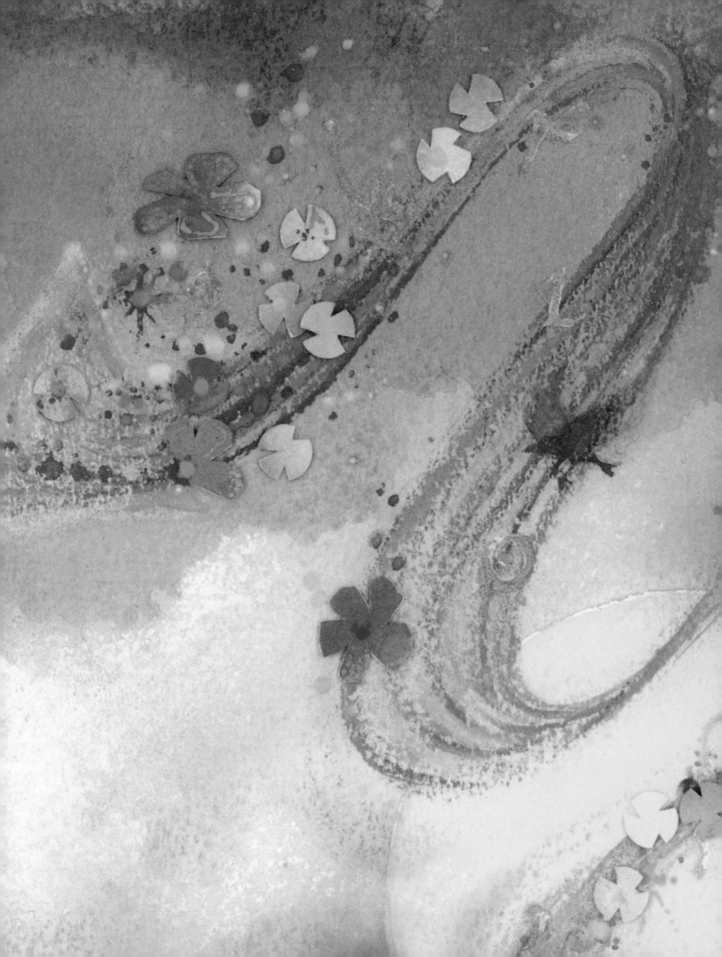

About the Author

Pᴀᴍᴇʟᴀ Gʀᴀғ Sʜᴏʀᴛ counts her farm heritage as one of the great blessings of her life. On the Ohio homestead, she was surrounded by neighbors who understood the value of blessing one another with fellowship, kindness, generosity, and laughter. Many blessings in this book flow from her childhood memories. Others are gleaned from her diverse vocational history as a nurse, a teacher of world religions, a pastor, and a mother. "I think I am correct in saying that the first formal blessing given to me as a babe was Numbers 6:24-26 (see previous page). And though blessed throughout my life, it was not until I read Dr. Rachel Naomi Remen's *My Grandfather's Blessings* that I really understood blessing as an unconditional gift of pure grace."

Pamela is an ordained minister in the Presbyterian Church, USA, serving Jesus Christ through the Maumee Valley Presbytery (Ohio and Michigan). She and husband Peter are grateful to count their family as blessings: Benjamin and Lauren, Allison and Andrew, grandsons Samuel, Isaac, Nathan, and Jaden, whose brief earthly life broke open a mighty waterfall of love.

About the Illustrator

GWEN STAMM, the oldest of six children, grew up on a farm near Archbold, Ohio. Besides raising turkeys, her family cared for their pets, including cats and dogs, instilling in Gwen a sensitivity for the well-being of animals and all creatures of the natural world.

In addition to work on the farm, Gwen and two of her sisters closest in age spent much time in their early years singing as a trio, playing, and drawing cut-out families together.

When she was age nine or ten, Gwen's mom and dad gave her a book of drawing instructions, a gift which has led her on a revelatory, vivid, colorful adventure of exploring with artistic creations ever since.

Gwen studied art and design at Hesston (Kansas) College and Bethel College in North Newton, Kansas. She worked as a graphic designer at Goshen (Indiana) College and Mennonite Publishing House in Scottdale, Pennsylvania. Currently, she does freelance and volunteer art, design, and calligraphy projects for clients and the church she attends. She's a member of the Calligraphy Guild of Pittsburgh, and occasionally attends calligraphy workshops which the guild offers.

Gwen lives in Scottdale, Pennsylvania, with her husband, Robert Eby, and their beloved orange tabby cat, Georgi.